DATE DUE

Ap 14/93			
MAR 16 95			
MAR 29 '95			
APR 28 18			
NO 12 02			
MR 21'06			

POTATOES

Dorothy Turner

Illustrations by John Yates

Carolrhoda Books, Inc./Minneapolis

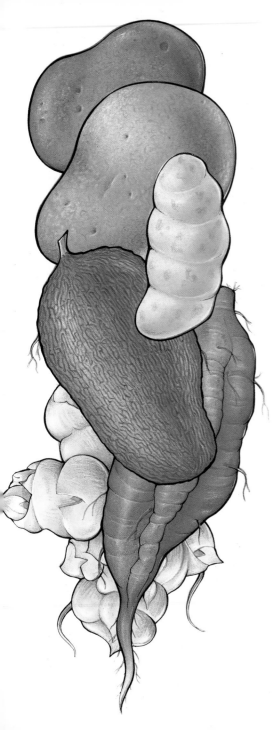

All words that appear in bold are
explained in the glossary on page 30.

First published in the U.S. in 1989 by
Carolrhoda Books, Inc.

Copyright © 1988 Wayland (Publishers) Ltd., Hove, East
Sussex. First published 1988 by Wayland (Publishers) Ltd.

Library of Congress Cataloging-in-Publication Data

Turner, Dorothy.
    Potatoes / Dorothy Turner ; illustrations by John Yates.
       p.   cm.
    Bibliography: p.
    Includes index.
    Summary: Describes the history, cultivation, and nutritional value
of the potato. Includes recipes, instructions for making potato
prints, and tips on how to grow your own potatoes.
    ISBN 0-87614-362-1 (lib. bdg.)
    1. Potatoes—Juvenile literature. [1. Potatoes.] I. Yates,
John, ill. II. Title.
SB211.P8T82   1988
633'.491—dc19   88-24156
                                                          CIP
                                                          AC

Printed in Italy by G. Canale C.S.p.A., Turin
Bound in the United States of America

1 2 3 4 5 6 7 8 9 10 99 98 97 96 95 94 93 92 91 90 89

Contents

Introducing the potato

potato

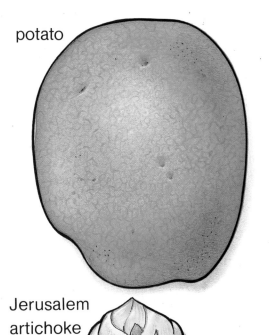

Jerusalem
artichoke

You already know that the potato is a vegetable, but did you realize that it is also a **tuber**? Tubers are fleshy underground parts of certain plants. They store food for the plant.

Potatoes aren't the only tubers. Two other tubers, the yam and the sweet potato, are as popular in tropical parts of the world as the potato is in North America and Europe. Other vegetables, such as Jerusalem artichokes and ocas, are tubers too.

oca

There are many different kinds of potatoes. In a supermarket in the United States, only 3 or 4 kinds may be for sale. But in a village market in South America, there might be as many as *60* types available.

Potato skins may be brownish white, pink, red, or even purple. The flesh inside may be white, yellow, or purple. Potato textures and flavors vary too. Some are soft and floury when cooked, and others are firm and waxy.

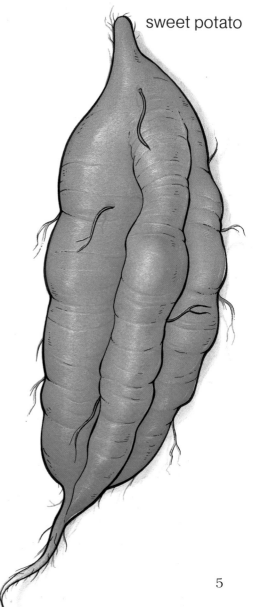

sweet potato

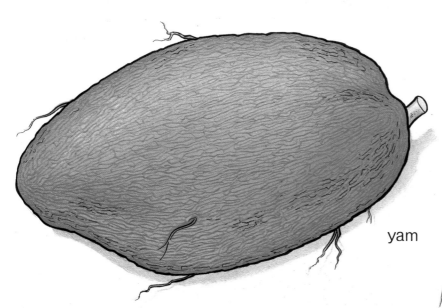

yam

Potatoes in our diet

Can you imagine life without potato chips, french fries, or baked potatoes? Why are potatoes so popular? Besides being easy to grow and cheap to buy, they can be used in many different ways. Most important, potatoes are a very good food.

Buying yams from a market stall on the Pacific island of New Caledonia

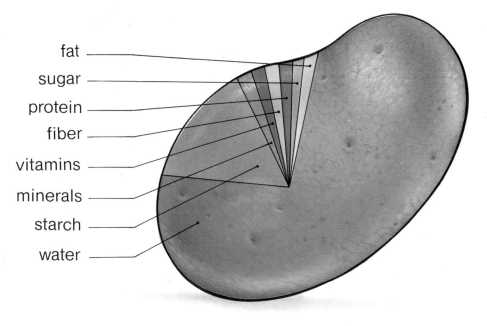

fat
sugar
protein
fiber
vitamins
minerals
starch
water

Left: A potato is made up of all these substances.

Below: South Pacific islanders celebrating a festival dedicated to yams

As you can see by the diagram, potatoes are mostly water. They also contain starch, fiber, vitamins, and minerals. People need all of these nutrients to stay healthy.

Potatoes are grown all over the world, but they grow best in cooler areas. Large amounts are grown in Europe, North and South America, the Soviet Union, Australia, and New Zealand. We talk about potatoes as if there were only one kind. In fact, there are more than 5,000 different kinds.

The history of potatoes

A Bolivian woman bakes potatoes outside, as people in the Andes have been doing for centuries.

Potatoes first grew in the Andes Mountains of South America, probably in Peru. Farmers there started cultivating them as long ago as 3000 B.C. The people baked bread using a light, powdery flour that they made from potatoes. But potatoes were unknown in the rest of the world until Spanish sailors brought them back to Europe

after exploring South America in the 16th century.

People in Europe, however, disliked the strange new vegetable. When people heard that they were supposed to eat the underground part of the plant, they thought it was a mistake, so they ate the leaves instead. This made them ill because the leaves contain a poisonous substance called solanine.

Some farmers and gardeners were successful at growing the new plant. But most people could not be persuaded to eat potatoes. They thought they were poisonous or caused disease. They even refused to eat the vegetable when they were starving.

For a long time, potatoes were looked down on in Europe. They were eaten only by very poor people or fed to farm animals. It was only about two hundred years ago that potatoes started to become popular.

Irish peasants plant potatoes under the watchful eye of an overseer.

In a part of Germany called Bavaria, the minister of war realized that the potato was an ideal food for his soldiers. It was cheap, nourishing, and easy to grow. He ordered the troops to plant potato patches. Soon, the potato was a great success.

Disease killed off most of the potato crop in Ireland in the 1840s. This farmer gazes in disbelief at his few tiny potatoes.

A hungry peasant family in their cottage. Many of the Irish starved during the potato famine.

Gradually, it became popular in other countries too.

In the early 19th century, Irish peasants depended on potatoes as their main food. When disease wiped out the Irish potato crop in 1845, two million people starved to death.

Today, potatoes are eaten by people all over the world. They may be called french fries at a hot dog stand or *pommes frites* in a fancy restaurant, but they are all made from the same vegetable.

How potatoes grow

Buds sprouting from the eyes of a potato

If you look carefully at a potato, you will see that it is covered with small dents, called **eyes**. On potatoes stored for a long time, these eyes form **buds**. The buds then **sprout**, or start to grow, and become new potato plants.

Farmers and gardeners, however, do not usually plant old sprouting potatoes. Instead, they plant

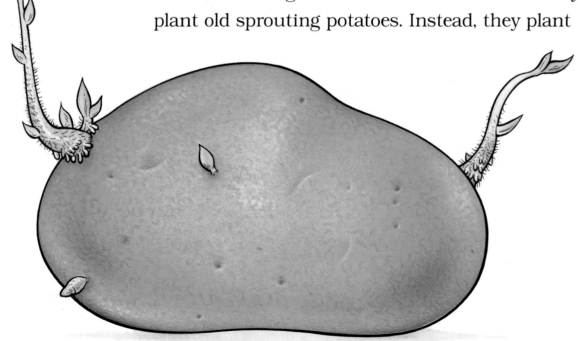

specially grown little potatoes called **seed potatoes**. Seed potatoes are raised to be disease-free so that farmers can be sure of a healthy crop.

When a seed potato is planted, the sprouts begin to develop. Long, thin roots grow down from the base and sides of the sprouts, and tiny leaves begin to form on the sprout tips.

At first, the new plant is fed by the **starch** stored inside the seed potato. When all the food is used up, the roots begin to absorb water and nutrients from the soil.

Planting seed potatoes in a field in England

Soon, the plant starts to flower. The flowers can be white, pink, or purple, depending on the kind of potato. The leaves use sunlight to make food for the plant. Some of the food is stored underground in the roots. These roots swell to form tubers called potatoes.

A plant may grow as many as 20 potatoes, but usually there are 3 to 6. When they are big enough to eat, the potatoes are dug up. Some potatoes

This potato plant has formed several tubers underground.

14

A field of potato plants in flower

grow to be more than six inches long and weigh as much as three pounds.

The flowers of two "parent" potato plants can produce seeds. These seeds, like the seed potatoes, can be used to grow potato plants. It takes longer to grow a plant using seeds.

Seeds are used to develop new kinds of potatoes. A potato plant grown from a seed will be different from both its parent plants. But a plant grown from a seed potato is exactly the same as the plant that made the seed potato.

Farming potatoes

Potatoes are grown in large, open fields. Before the potatoes are planted, **fertilizer** is added to the soil. Next, long, narrow **furrows**, or ruts, are dug by machine. Then another machine plants seed potatoes in the furrows at regular spaces. In some countries, this work is still done by hand.

If the tubers of a potato plant are exposed

Oxen are being used to plow this potato field in Nepal.

Left: A farmer plowing furrows with a tractor

Below: Seed potatoes are fed by hand into this machine, which then plants them in the furrows.

to sunlight as they grow, they turn green and taste bitter. So farmers make sure they stay covered by piling up soil at the base of each potato plant.

When the plants have flowered, the potatoes are **harvested,** or dug up. Any that are green, diseased, shriveled, or damaged by insects are thrown away. The good ones are then sorted according to size.

Farmers store potatoes in cool, dark places. Potatoes can be kept from spoiling for as long as a year after they are harvested.

Harvesting potatoes by hand in Bolivia

Sorting freshly harvested potatoes

Nowadays, potatoes are packed in plastic bags to be sold. Potatoes will last longer if you take them out of the bag and store them in a cool, dark place.

Potato products

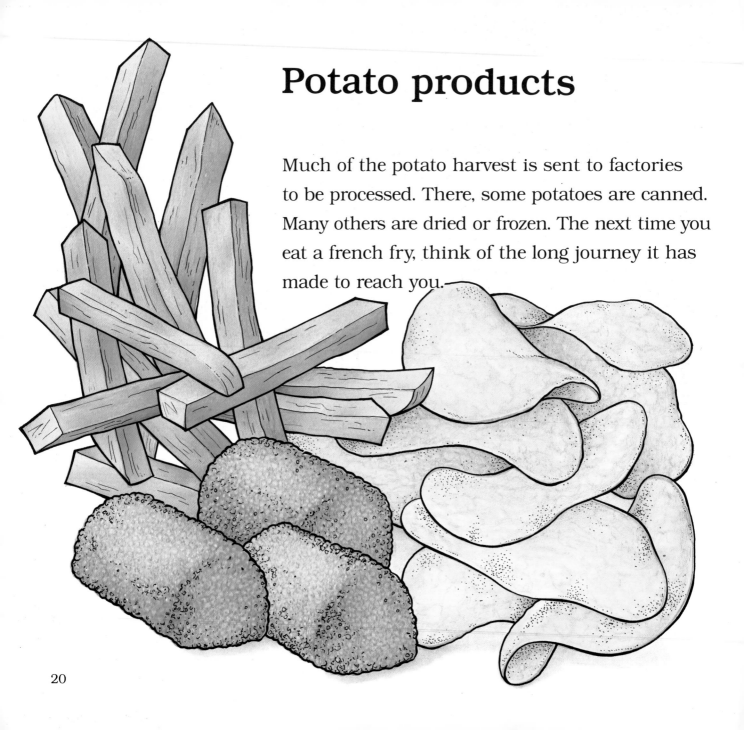

Much of the potato harvest is sent to factories to be processed. There, some potatoes are canned. Many others are dried or frozen. The next time you eat a french fry, think of the long journey it has made to reach you.

Potato chips are also made at factories. The potatoes are cut into thin slices. Then the slices are fried and salted, and sometimes special flavorings, such as garlic or onion, are added.

Grow your own potatoes

In the spring, buy some seed potatoes from a garden center or a plant nursery. Stand them up in egg cartons. Make sure the end with the most eyes is at the top. Keep them in a light, cool spot away from direct sunlight.

When they sprout, keep only three good, strong **shoots** on each potato. Rub off all the others.

Dig a trench in soil that has been fertilized. Make it about six inches deep. Plant the seed

A young girl from Nepal digs up potatoes that have been stored underground.

potatoes about a foot apart. If you have several rows, keep the rows two feet apart.

You can also grow potatoes in flowerpots. Choose a pot that measures at least eight inches across, to give the plant plenty of room to grow. Keep the pot in a sunny place.

Water the plants well, and remove any weeds that sprout up. As your plants grow, pile up soil around them. This makes sure the potatoes will develop in the dark.

After the plants have flowered, dig up the potatoes as you want them.

How to make potato prints

You will need: potatoes knife paints paper

Be careful not to cut yourself with the knife when you are carving the potato.

Cut a potato in half. Then cut a pattern into the cut side of the potato. You can choose any design you like.

Dip the cut side of the potato into the paint. Now you can print the pattern over and over again. Experiment with different colors and

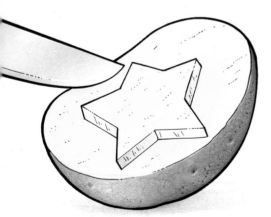

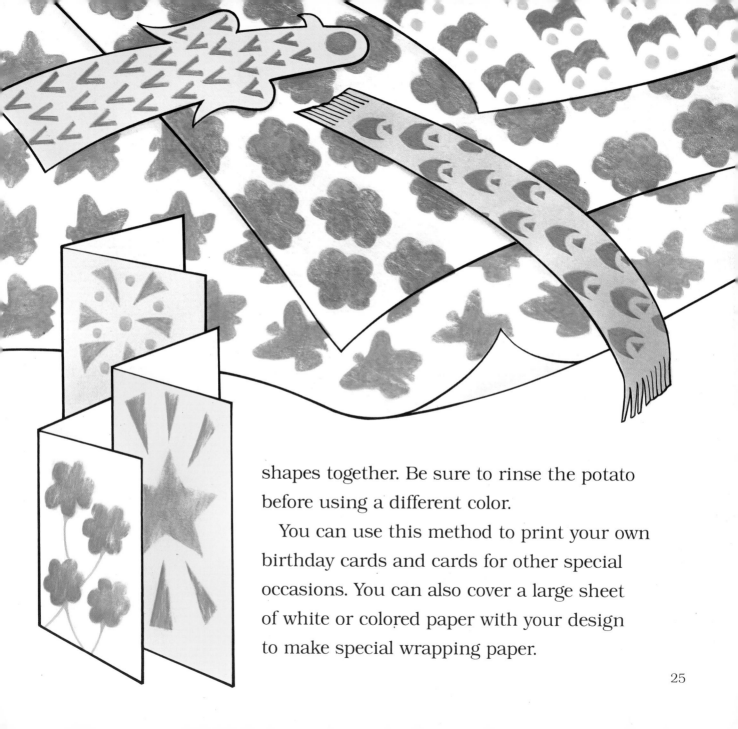

shapes together. Be sure to rinse the potato before using a different color.

You can use this method to print your own birthday cards and cards for other special occasions. You can also cover a large sheet of white or colored paper with your design to make special wrapping paper.

25

Cooking

Potatoes can be boiled, steamed, fried, baked, or roasted. The most nutritious part of a potato lies just under the skin, so it is healthiest to eat them unpeeled. Unpeeled potatoes should be well scrubbed.

Baked potatoes

You will need:

4 medium potatoes
cooking oil
topping (see list below)

1. Scrub the potatoes. Prick them with a fork, and lightly brush them with oil.

2. Bake at 420°F for 1-1½ hours or until potatoes can be easily pierced with a fork.

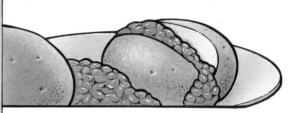

3. When cooked, cut them open and serve with your favorite topping. Here are some to try:

· butter
· gravy
· butter and grated cheese
· sour cream and chives
· cottage cheese and bacon
· broccoli and melted cheese
· chili and melted cheese
· mushrooms
· fried onions

Pommes Anna

(a French recipe)

You will need:

4 potatoes
⅓ cup butter
salt and pepper

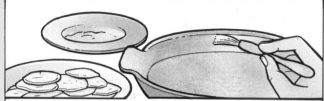

1. Peel the potatoes and slice them very thinly. Melt butter and brush it on the sides of a round ovenproof dish.

2. Layer potatoes in the dish, sprinkling each layer with salt and pepper.

3. Pour more melted butter over the top.

4. Cook at 400°F for 1 hour or until potatoes are tender.

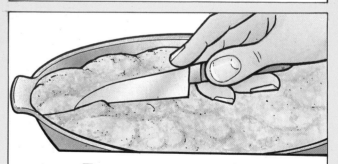

5. To serve, cut into slices like a cake.

East Indian potatoes

You will need:

4 medium potatoes
3 tablespoons cooking oil
1 teaspoon whole cumin seeds
1 tablespoon whole sesame seeds
1 teaspoon black mustard seeds
1 teaspoon salt
a pinch of cayenne pepper
1 tablespoon lemon juice

1. Boil potatoes in their skins until they can be pierced with a fork. Let them cool. Peel skins off, and cut potatoes into cubes about ¾ inch in size.

2. Heat the oil in a wok or a large frying pan. When it is hot, add all the seeds. In a few moments, the seeds will pop.

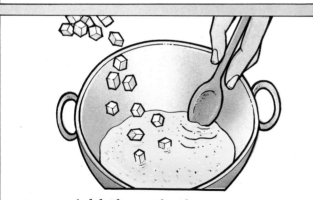

3. Add the cubed potatoes. Stir well, and fry for about 5 minutes.

4. Add the salt, cayenne pepper, and lemon juice. Fry, stirring often, for about 3 more minutes. Eat alone or serve with meat.

Glossary

buds: small structures, such as those that grow out of the eyes on a potato, that can sprout and grow into a plant

eyes: small dents on a potato

fertilizer: nutrients added to the soil to help plants grow

furrows: long, narrow cuts in the ground in which plants are sowed

harvest: gather a crop

seed potatoes: specially grown potatoes planted to grow new potato plants

shoot: new plant growth

sprout: start to grow

starch: a form in which plants store food

tuber: the fleshy part of a plant that grows
   underground. It is the part of the potato plant
   that we eat.

Index

Photo Acknowledgments

The photographs in this book were provided by: p. 6, Christine Osborne; pp. 7, 8, 16, 18, 23, The Hutchison Library; pp. 9, 10, Mary Evans Picture Library; p. 11, The Mansell Collection; pp. 13, 17 (left), 19, Potato Marketing Board; pp. 15, 17 (bottom) Holt Studios; p. 24, P. Seheult/Wayland Picture Library.